The Truth Will Set You Free,
But First It Will Piss You Off!

RANDOM HOUSE • NEW YORK

Gloria Steinem
The Truth Will Set You Free,
But First It Will Piss You Off!

Thoughts on Life, Love, and Rebellion

Illustrations by Samantha Dion Baker

*This book is dedicated
to Amy Richards,
without whose smarts
it wouldn't exist*

CONTENTS

The Poetry of Everyday Life

Somewhere between poetry and journalism lies the magical land of quotes. They may be fact or fantasy, personal or political, from academia or the street, but they are smart enough to be memorable and short enough to remember.

You might say they are the poetry of everyday life.

A quote can turn a tweet into a haiku because it evokes a story. Indeed, if you poured water on a quote, it would *become* a story. "Tell me a fact and I'll forget," as a Native American quote goes, "but tell me a story and I'll always remember."

If a quote evokes more than one story, it's likely to last a very long time.

Take the first half of the title of this book: "The truth will set you free." That was said by Jesus in the Bible, and the truth was the Word of God. Academics used the same quote to say that knowledge would set you free. Then during the war in Vietnam, young men wrote that quote on protest signs, hoping that the truth of the war would set them free from the draft.

It was then that I added, "But first it will piss you off." That's because I was pretty sure we were not only in the wrong war, we were also on the wrong side.

If this sounds far out even now, let me tell you a story of my own.

I lived in India for a couple of years after college, and I learned that Ho Chi Minh, our enemy-to-be in Vietnam, was a much-admired anticolonial hero whose model for getting the French out of his country was the American Revolution. He also risked his life to rescue our pilots downed in the jungle during World War II, and he impressed them by reciting our entire Declaration of Independence by heart.

With the hope of making a human connection to a man who was supposed to be our enemy, I researched, wrote, and published an essay about Ho Chi Minh. I have to say this had no public impact at all. I also learned that some veterans who knew and liked Ho Chi Minh during the war had gone to Washington to plead the case. They had no impact either.

I felt pissed off and powerless, as if I were living in an alternate universe. On my bulletin board, I put this quote of my own: "Alienation is when your country is at war, and you want the other side to win."

Soon more truths of the war began to come out of hiding. Our government had been concealing death statistics in order to downplay our casualties, exaggerate Ho Chi Minh's casualties, and make the war seem under control. Before the end came, thousands of Americans would lose their lives on the battlefield, and more from Agent Orange and Vietnam-related damage to their spirits and bodies, plus millions of Vietnamese soldiers and civilians in both north and south.

Eventually, the sheer number of Americans marching and opposing the war forced President Lyndon Johnson to resign and President Richard Nixon to preside over our retreat. Vietnam became the first war this country ever lost.

But movements don't only create change in the outside world, they transform people in them. Many women had organized against Vietnam—and for civil rights, against nuclear testing, and more—so they learned they could have a public impact. Yet they also learned that even in those idealistic movements, women were not treated as equals by many of the men.

This pissed a lot of women off. I began to see feminist slogans, including the title of this book, which I thought no one had noticed, on T-shirts and buttons, bulletin boards, campus banners, and even sidewalks as graffiti.

There also turned out to be a parallel to this title in programs for and by alcoholics: "The truth will set you free, but first it will make you miserable." Is this related? I have no idea.

It's always honorable to credit the source of a quote, which also helps to explain its meaning, but claiming ownership of a quote is often beside the point. We all contribute to the collective unconscious from which quotes come.

Even all these decades after this quote emerged in the peace and feminist movements, I see the hybrid title of this book on posters and painted on the side of a truck, in demonstrations, online, in needlepoint, and even as a tattoo. In tragedies, we might now also say, the truth will set you free—but first it will make you mourn. Alice Walker always reminds me of that.

As I write this, for instance, I've just returned from speaking in the grand old Castro Theatre in San Francisco, together with artist and activist Favianna Rodriguez. Though I don't remember either of us repeating this quote during our talk, a young hijab-wearing woman in the audience came up afterward to say that it was her favorite, and that she had translated it into Persian and Kurdish for her feminist blog in Iran. Why? Because it applied to women's lives there.

Who would have guessed? She was a reminder that quotes go global.

Even before the World Wide Web, quotes were contagious. Almost fifty years ago, Simone de Beauvoir and other women in France wrote "I have had an abortion" on a petition, demanded the repeal of antiabortion laws, and gathered hundreds of signatures. In the first issue of *Ms.* magazine, we followed their example with a petition signed by hundreds of women in the United States. It was this shared and personal quote that made all the difference.

More than a decade ago in this country, Tarana Burke, herself a survivor of sexual assault, was working to help young girls survive abuse, and coined "Me too" as a way of sharing the personal experience of sexual assault. Women picked this quote up by the millions to share their experiences on social media.

Then women in Hollywood came forward with stories of their own sexual harassment by men who could make or break their careers. They declared, "Time's up!" This wave of truth-telling began reverberating around the country, from women farm workers and restaurant workers to students, gymnasts, and more.

"Me too" and "Time's up!" have also spread around the world as contagious movements, from India's glamorous Bollywood to students and workers in Seoul, London, and Nairobi. Such shared quotes are the most powerful and contagious path to change because each one contains a personal story.

In a way, passing on a quote is like putting a note in a bottle and sending it out to sea. You may never know who will find your words—or who said or wrote the words you may find—but each quote is an entry in the diary of humankind. Without such honest words, that diary would be incomplete.

• • •

We are again in a time of crisis and dissent, just as we were when the hybrid title of this book was inspired by

Vietnam protest signs. As I write this, even more Americans are opposed to this occupant of the White House, and the marches and demonstrations are even more widespread. They go beyond ending the draft or an unjust war. Now they challenge how our leaders are elected, who is allowed into this country and who is cast out, what are facts and what are not, and whether every citizen's vote counts.

That last point may be the key to all the others. Donald Trump, who is the occupant of the White House at this moment, lost the 2016 election by nearly eleven million votes, three million for Hillary Clinton and eight million for other candidates—a far bigger popular vote loss than any president in history. He succeeded only because of the Electoral College, a system of weighted voting that the southern slave-owning states wrote into the Constitution at this country's founding. Only five times in U.S. history have the electoral and popular verdicts been different, but there has always been the possibility of straying far from one person, one vote. Because of the Electoral College, the voting power of a citizen in Wyoming, the least populated state, is 3.6 times that of a citizen in the largest state, California.

I don't like to cite a problem without suggesting a solution, so even though this is not a quote, let me say that, since the 1940s, public opinion polls have shown that an overwhelming majority of Americans want to eliminate the Electoral College and to be assured of one citizen, one vote. There just hasn't been enough energy or urgency to undertake the long process of passing a constitutional amendment to get rid of the Electoral College, but now there is another way to equalize voting power. State legislatures are voting to give all their states' electoral votes to the candidate who wins the national majority vote. Once this number of states passes the tipping point and represents more than half of all electoral votes, the Electoral College will become obsolete. This initiative is known as the National Popular Vote Interstate Compact.

Has the truth of Trump's unpopular election pissed off enough state representatives to set us free from the Electoral College? Has it pissed off enough voters to force them to do it? As I'm writing this, the answer is blowing in the wind.

But sometimes the lessons of defeat can be even more important than a passing victory. We are learning a lot due to the disaster of an unelected president in the White House, from the depth of remaining racism to the unearned economic influence of the wealthy few.

And we're learning how to fight without repeating the tactics of our adversaries. For instance, if there were a Nobel Prize for the right quote at the right time, it would go to Michelle Obama for saying to the whole country, "When they go low, we go high." We don't win by imitating what we're against.

We're also learning that the most dangerous time often comes after a victory. For instance, a peace movement ended the Vietnam War by popular demand, and the civil rights, feminist, gay, lesbian, transgender, and environmental movements have now changed the majority consciousness of this nation. But these majority changes have left about a third of the country feeling deprived of the hierarchies they grew up with: white over black, men over women, people over nature, monotheism over spirituality, heterosexual over all other forms of love—and the list goes on.

When I'm traveling, I'm often confronted by a middle-aged white man who says something like "A black woman took my job." My answer is always "Who said it was your job?" The problem is his sense of entitlement.

Yet we have too often celebrated progress and not understood the dangers of an earlier majority becoming a minority. There are plenty of examples.

For instance, the crime of lynching became commonplace not during slavery but after emancipation, when white racists feared the new voting and economic power of black Americans. The Civil War had eliminated slavery but hadn't challenged the power of racism.

Another example: Not until after World War II did the U.S. government make propaganda films that glorified white women in suburban kitchens. That's because once the war was over, women who had been working in war factories, or were otherwise independent, were supposed to go home, leave their jobs to men, and, as housewives, become full-time consumers whose endless buying and suburban lifestyle would replace the economic engine of the war.

Similarly, even when abortions were illegal, women who had them were not threatened with the death penalty. But Texas, Ohio, and perhaps by now other states are responding to decades of women having the power to decide the fate of their own bodies by proposing legislation that has included the death penalty for women who have abortions and loss of license or prison for the doctors. That was too extreme to pass, but so-called heartbeat bills criminalize abortion for both woman and physician long before a fetus could possibly survive outside a woman's body. These bills are succeeding even though they put women's bodies and the practice of medicine under government control.

This backlash is also fueled by the imminent change of this country's majority from white people to people of color. Indeed, the first generation that is majority babies of color has already been born. This is a great thing for our country in a post-colonial and striving to become post-racist age, but it is also energizing a racist and anti-immigrant reaction. For instance, the depth of white racism and antifeminism can be seen in "replacement theory," a white nationalist effort to persuade, reward, or otherwise force white women to have more white children. This is also a motivation of the antiabortion movement.

Altogether, there is a backlash against the social justice movements that have changed majority conscious-

ness from the 1960s forward. Public opinion polls now show that most Americans no longer approve of laws based on race, gender, ethnicity, sexuality, and other group judgments. We are more likely to see each other as unique individuals as well as universally human. To cite a quote from this book, more of us understand that "we are linked, not ranked."

That is a cause for celebration—and also caution.

Just as the family is the source of everything from violence to democracy, it is also the source of a lesson here. For a woman in a violent household, the most dangerous time is just before or just after she escapes. This is when she is most likely to be injured or killed. Why? Because she is escaping control. She is about to be free.

The majority in this country are escaping control of old

hierarchies of race and gender and more. This means two things:

First, we need to be aware of the danger and look after each other.

Second, just as we would never tell a woman to go back to a violent household, we too will not go back to the past.

We may be about to be free.

. . .

There are also quotes that no longer have relevance. I think it's called growing up. For instance, I used to say, "The examined life is not worth living." It was obviously a reversal of what Socrates said when he was on trial for his life: "The unexamined life is not worth living."

My version was a smartass way of saying that I could live an activist life forever, without admitting how my unchosen childhood patterns were still magnets in my supposedly chosen adult life.

Until you de-magnetize whatever early patterns you inherited, you are probably making choices that aren't really yours. Socrates knew what he was talking about.

I also had a deep and not totally unfounded fear of becoming a bag lady. After all, I was freelancing and had never saved a penny in my life. I dealt with this fear by saying, "If I become a bag lady, I'll just organize the other bag ladies—it's a life like any other."

I doubt this unrealism was shared by real bag ladies. They probably would have liked a room of their own, and preferred the street only because it was less dangerous than overcrowded shelters.

But once I passed fifty and actually began to save money for the first time ever, this romance with becoming a bag lady gradually disappeared. I unpacked the boxes that had been a feature of my apartment when it was just a stop on the road. I created a home.

One more quote I have abandoned over the years: "Men should think twice before making widowhood women's only path to power." Once, women's main path to power was widowhood. Even Senator Margaret Chase Smith, who became a hero by facing down Senator Joe McCarthy, inherited her office from her husband. Thankfully, in this new era, women are powerful on their own, independent of who they are attached to.

• • •

I hope you find encouragement and company in this lifetime collection of quotes from my speeches, articles, and books, plus some from my friends. I've chosen the ones that I hope will be the most useful in arguments, the most comforting in bad times, and the most inspirational when needed, as well as the most likely to lead to laughter.

At the end of the book, I've left space so that you can write down your own quotes or those you find and want to save.

For me, coming up with a good quote is like being in an editorial meeting where everyone is searching for ideas, words are flying through the air, and then finding a sudden *aha!* That's high praise because my idea of heaven is an editorial meeting.

On these pages, I've tried to pretend we were in such a meeting together.

A quote is the essence of a story. We all need stories to convey ideas, justice, anger, humanity, hope, laughter, learning, and whatever makes us understand or feel understood.

We all need words that tell our own story. I hope you find some here.

The Truth Will Set You Free,
But First It Will Piss You Off!

CHAPTER 1

Families Born and Chosen

Each of us is a unique result of millennia of heredity and environment combined in a way that could never have happened before and can never happen again. Families should be the place to see and welcome us as unique individuals. It doesn't matter whether they are biological or created by adoption, whether they consist of one person or many, as long as they accept us and love us as we are.

No child arrives as a blank slate. You might say that we need families that help us become who we already are. Yet too many families still treat children as if they are blank slates on which parents can write their own hopes or frustrated dreams.

Instead, try thinking of families as gardens. If we arrive as a petunia in a garden of roses and lilies, we probably will need a friend, a neighbor, a teacher, or a grandmother—someone who knows a petunia when she sees one and helps us to bloom as ourselves. And there is always hope. As the poet Alice Walker wrote in *Revolutionary Petunias*, "the nature of this flower is to bloom."

Birth families have the purpose not only of nurturing,

but of bringing family members together with people they might never otherwise have known or accepted—or even liked. Dorothy Dinnerstein, a very wise philosopher, once said that a crucial purpose of birth families is to make sure we know, value, and even love people we don't agree with. Learning to accept and even love difference, as she pointed out, is important for the future of the human race. There is great comfort in realizing that differences within a family have an important purpose.

As we human beings grow up, our time of dependency lasts far longer than that of any other animal. That's because our very complex brains continue to add countless synapses over the years.

The good news is that this long process gives our brains the power to adapt to almost any environment, so our species survives. The bad news is that this same process makes us vulnerable to everything around us, from the absence of touch to the presence of disapproval. We are hypersensitive to whatever is normalized or enforced while we are young.

Imagine how vulnerable we are to our treatment and surroundings as we grow up. Whether we are born into a family or adopted, whether we live in poverty or in a mansion, with a single mother or two fathers, what children absorb is: Who speaks and who listens? Who argues and who gives in? Who is at the computer and who is in the kitchen? Who is the family proud of, and who isn't mentioned? Who brings worry, and who brings hope? Families that preach gender and race equality but don't practice it cannot advance equality. They just teach us to separate our words from our deeds.

On the other hand, chosen families are people who share and support our hopes and interests. We need and choose our friends, colleagues, co-workers, lovers, and partners because we are communal animals. If we are alone for long, we come to feel uncertain or wrong. It doesn't matter whether our chosen family takes the form of a weekly lunch group or an office professional group or a revolutionary feminist cell. We all need people we trust, who understand us and will tell us when we're messing up, who support us and celebrate when we reach a personal goal. This is our chosen family.

People have been sitting around a communal campfire for most of human history, learning from others' stories and telling our own. Without a chosen family of shared values and hope, we will surely feel alone and defeated.

• • •

It's easy to see why democracy starts in our birth family. Yet it's not so easy to find political philosophers who begin their thinking with families. Even advocates of gender equality in the larger world seem to stop their theorizing at the family door. They may accept or just not comment on households in which mothers do most or all of the caregiving, and men do or don't give financial support. On the pretext of public versus private, they talk about democracy as if it were a tree without roots. Democracy is the tree, families are the roots.

I fear that those who oppose democracy are way smarter. They start by opposing women's control of our reproductive lives. They know that our ability to make this very decision—whether to have children or not—is the biggest determinant of whether we are healthy or not, educated or not, employed outside the home or not, and how long we live. Even for women who have some role in public life, the patriarchal family often remains the microcosm of an authoritarian state.

No one could have been clearer about the political importance of a patriarchal family of birth than the rising Adolf Hitler. As he warned in *Mein Kampf*, "It must be considered as reprehensible conduct to refrain from giving healthy children to the nation." Among his first acts were to padlock family planning clinics and to declare abortion a crime against the state. Punishment was prison and hard labor for the woman, who then could be forced to bear children, and death for the doctor.

To transform inequality in the outside world, we have to start inside the home. We have to get rid of the old idea that what happens to men is political, and therefore subject to change, but what happens to women is cultural, and therefore can't, or shouldn't, be changed.

Once, when early feminists Robin Morgan, Shulamith Firestone, and Pat Mainardi were having a discussion

about the politics of women's lives, Robin, being a poet, brought it all together in the simple quote: "The personal is political." It's hard to think of another quote that has transformed so much and informed so many.

A half-century later a woman's position is now understood to be political and changeable, even by people who oppose changing it. And "the personal is political" has become part of everyday language.

Movements are chosen families, just on a larger scale. We need a movement that is as diverse as the people impacted by the change we seek. That means we must embody the ends we want.

For instance, I can't imagine life without a local, national, and global feminist movement that protects and instructs, shares ideas and knowledge, tells us when we're

Revolutions, like trees, Grow from the bottom up.

messing up, provides a global network of co-conspirators, regroups after defeats, and dances after victories.

In practice, there are links of cause and effect between birth families and chosen families, and also between movement change and global change.

For instance, in *Sex and World Peace,* Valerie Hudson and other scholars conducted a study of violence in a hundred nations around the world. The single biggest determinant of whether a nation would be violent, both in its own streets and in military violence against another country, was domestic violence in the home. More than poverty, access to natural resources, religion, or even degree of democracy, they found that violence against females was the indicator and normalizer of all other violence.

This starts with male control of reproduction, and therefore the bodies of women. Since half the population cannot control the other half without violence or the threat of violence, male-dominant cultures lead us to believe that such control and violence are inevitable and even natural.

Yet long ago and still, there are examples to the contrary. For instance, think of the difference between the extreme gender polarization of terrorist groups and the porous and flexible gender roles of more peaceful and democratic groups and nations, from Sweden to Kerala in southern India. The less gender-polarized the culture, the lower the degree of violence and the greater the degree of democracy.

As usual, everything grows like a tree: from the bottom up.

A nomad follows the
seasons and the animals,
taking family along.
I followed a movement,
and found my family.

Perhaps the most revolutionary act and reward for a woman is a self-willed journey— and a welcome when she returns.

. . .

I sometimes wonder if I am crisscrossing my father's ghostly paths, and he and I are entering the same town, or roadside diner, or black ribbon of highway that gleams in the night rain. We are like images in a time-lapse photograph.

In many languages, even the word for human being is "one who goes on migrations."

. . .

Perhaps our need to escape through media is a misplaced desire for the journey.

. . .

We need to make chosen families of small groups of women who support each other, talk to each other regularly, can speak their truths and their experiences, and find they're not alone in them. It makes all the difference.

We need each other. We are all passengers
on Spaceship Earth.

• • •

I wish you work that you would want to do even
if you weren't paid, and friends who are chosen
family. Then you can withstand all the storms
of life and become who you uniquely are.

• • •

My love of community came from a
movement.

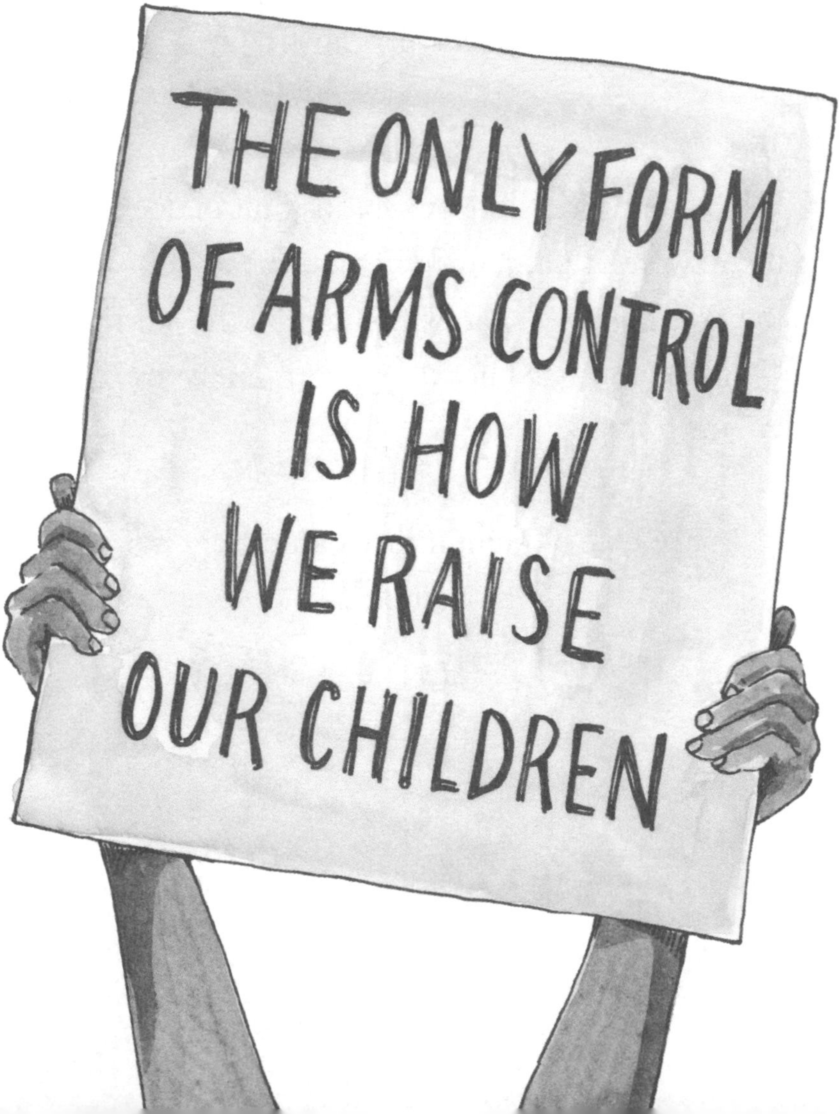
THE ONLY FORM
OF ARMS CONTROL
IS HOW
WE RAISE
OUR CHILDREN

As long as females are valued only for our wombs, we will never be valued for our minds and hearts.

. . .

So many of us are living out the unlived lives of our mothers.

. . .

Childbirth is more admirable than conquest, more amazing than self-defense, and as courageous as either one.

. . .

I have very little faith in heredity, and a lot of faith in the power of who raises us.

mother as a verb.

Mother (verb): to be, to think, to love, to do.

In thinking about Mother's Day, why do I and others who are not mothers identify with this day just as much as if we were?

Of course, it's partly because we all owe our lives to our own *mothers*—which would be enough—but I think there is another reason. Even if we are not *mothers*, the noun, we may be *mothering*, the verb. Indeed, unless *mothering* is a verb, it is not an action in the world.

Think about it: As a noun, *mother* is limited to half the human race, and also to the accident of fertility and age and intention. In some societies, motherhood is honored only in women who are married or who have sons. In most societies, a woman is encouraged to give birth to another person more than she is encouraged to give birth to herself.

As a noun, *mother* may be good or bad, willing or unwilling, on welfare or rich, worshipped or blamed, dominating or nurturing, accidental or chosen.

Perhaps that's why the word *mother* is so much used in profanity, as in *motherfucking;* in war, as in *the mother of all bombs*; or by warmakers who honor hero mothers who give birth to soldiers.

But when *mother* is a verb—as in *to be mothered* and *to mother*—ah, then the very best of human possibilities come into our imaginations.

To mother is to care about the welfare of another person as much as one's own.

To mother depends on empathy and thoughtfulness, noticing and caring.

To mother creates the only pairing in which the older and the younger, the strong and the weak are perfectly matched.

Mothering is also about free will. One can be forced to become a mother, but one cannot be forced *to mother*.

What Julia Ward Howe had in mind in 1870 when she invented Mother's Day for Peace was a day on which we oppose war and advance peace. In other words, it was not Mother's Day but Mothering Day. It reminds us all, whether we are young or old, male or female, of the possibilities that lie within us as human beings.

WHEN THE PILL CAME ALONG MORE WOMEN WERE ABLE TO GIVE BIRTH TO THEMSELVES.

Women can't *have* it all if that
means *doing* it all.

. . .

If a woman spends a year bearing and
nursing a child, why isn't a man responsible
for spending half the time plus another year
raising a child? Logic is in the eye of the
logician.

. . .

We need to remember across generations that
there is as much to learn as there is to teach.

A weed is just a flower that no one loves.

• • •

The best thing about self-defense is knowing
there is a self worth defending.

• • •

Self-esteem isn't everything; it's just that
there's nothing without it.

• • •

To write is to bring an inner voice into the
outer world, to believe that our thoughts are
worth entering the thinking of others, and to
make real what has never existed in quite the
same way before. What could be a better path
to self-value than that?

MY MOTHER ALWAYS SAID:
Democracy is just something
you do every day, like
brushing your teeth.

Democracy begins in the family.

But really, we could change *Democracy* to *Violence, Empathy*—anything. What happens in the family doesn't stay in the family. And I don't just mean the biological family, I mean whoever we live with and trust. If that trust is broken by violence or abuse, it takes generations to heal.

And likewise we could add:

Democracy begins with owning our bodies.
By that measure, women have rarely lived in
a democracy.

If you don't vote, you don't count.

. . .

THE VOTING BOOTH IS
THE ONE PLACE ON EARTH
WHERE THE LEAST POWERFUL
AND THE MOST POWERFUL
ARE EQUAL.

. . .

Saying politics is dirty is just a way of
keeping us from changing the politics of our
own lives.

THERE CAN BE NO
TRUE DEMOCRACY *with*
RACISM OR *without*
FEMINISM.

It's not only that we live in a patriarchy, it's that patriarchy lives in us.

. . .

I've learned feminism disproportionately from black women.

Because of racism, the white middle-class part of the movement got reported more, but look at the numbers. In 1972, in the very first national poll of women responding to feminist issues, African American women were twice as likely to support feminism and feminist issues as were white women. In 2016, 94 percent of black women voted for Hillary Clinton, and 52 percent of white women voted for Donald Trump.

. . .

It's not only that racism is all around us, it's that racism is in us.

The ability to live in the present, to tolerate uncertainty, and to remain open, spontaneous, and flexible are all culturally female qualities that many men have been denied.

• • •

Each of us has only one thing to gain from the feminist movement: our whole humanity.

• • •

Gender has wrongly told us that some things are masculine and some things are feminine . . . which is bullshit.

• • •

Women have to learn how to talk as much as we listen. Men have to learn how to listen as much as they talk.

• • •

If you have more power than others, remember to listen as much as you talk. If you have less power than others, remember to talk as much as you listen. This is instant democracy.

The Golden Rule was written by a smart guy for guys, but women need to reverse it:

TREAT OURSELVES AS WELL AS WE TREAT OTHERS.

The feminization of poverty equals the masculinization of wealth.

• • •

What happens to men is called *politics*. What happens to women is called *culture*.

It's one of the marks of matrilineal, egalitarian, original cultures that after marriage, the man joins the woman's household. It's a mark of male-dominant societies that the woman, sometimes even as a very young girl, joins her husband's household.

For five thousand years, women have been immigrants— but that is only five percent of human history. It's time that women were immigrants no more, but considered to have and deserve a home wherever they are.

Be sure
you like
who you
love.

Many are looking for the right person. Too few are trying to be the right person.

• • •

Love and power are opposites.

• • •

Someone once asked me why women don't gamble as much as men do. I gave the commonsense answer that we don't have as much money. Then I realized that until recently, our total instinct for gambling has been satisfied by marriage.

• • •

Marriage has worked better for men than for women. The two happiest groups are married men and unmarried women.

Women have been trained to measure our effectiveness in love and approval. That makes it tough to be personally independent or to advocate basic change.

• • •

Men can be just as loving and nurturing as women—it's a libel on men to say they can't—but we all learn by example. Boys just need nurturing men in their lives so they know it's okay for them to be nurturing.

• • •

If more men gained sensitive listening skills, they would have "intuition" too.

• • •

Women are not going to be equal outside the home until men are equal inside it.

• • •

Love is wanting what's best for the other person. *Romance* is wanting the other person.

WOMEN ARE BECOMING THE MEN WE WANTED TO MARRY.

(BUT TOO FEW MEN ARE BECOMING THE WOMEN THEY WANTED TO MARRY)

Whatever the superior group has will be used as proof of its superiority. Thus, if men could menstruate, it would become a great thing. Without this inbuilt measure of time and the movements of the universe, how could any woman become a mathematician? An astronomer?

• • •

Untangling sex from aggression and violence is going to take a very long time. It's a challenge to the very heart of male dominance.

• • •

All the qualities that are wrongly called "feminine" are really only qualities necessary to raise children: patience, nurturing, attention to detail, empathy. When men raise children, they develop these qualities too.

• • •

There are two reasons why people don't support the word *feminist*: The first is they *don't* know what it means. The second is they *do* know what it means.

"Every child has the right to be born loved and wanted."

This has been one of the most important arguments for letting women decide when and whether to give birth.

• • •

For women, home is more dangerous than the road.

Whether by dowry murders in India, honor killings in Egypt, or domestic violence in the United States, statistics show that women are most likely to be beaten or killed at home by men they know.

• • •

For 95 percent of human history, women decided when and whether to have children, and understood the use of herbs, abortifacients, and timing.

It took centuries of patriarchy, including the murder of six million "witches," healthcare wise women, to impose this control of women's bodies that is the first step in every hierarchy.

If they have dependent children, many women are one man away from welfare.

• • •

Whenever women have been valued for our heads and hearts as well as our wombs, and allowed to decide when and whether to give birth, population has settled at just a little over replacement level.

• • •

If women can't control our lives from the skin in, we can't control our lives from the skin out.

INVADING BODIES

is still less punished
than invading property.

. . .

What our bodies can do is way more
important than how they look.
Sports help young women realize that our
bodies are instruments, not ornaments.

Your daughters are watching you.

. . .

Every time a woman looks in a mirror and
criticizes her body, a girl is watching.

Like so many daughters who don't yet know that a female fate is not a personal fault, I told myself as a young woman, "I'm not going to be anything like my mother."

• • •

When people say to me, "What should I tell my daughter?" I always say: The most important thing is to listen. This is how she learns she has something to say.

• • •

Many people have begun to raise daughters more like sons, but too few people raise sons more like daughters.

The BEST way to cultivate FEARLESSNESS in our daughters and other young women is by EXAMPLE.

If in our earliest, most intimate world we grow callous to a power difference among our own family members, how much easier will it be for us to accept all other hierarchies?

• • •

Only after I saw women who were attracted to distant, condescending, even violent men did I begin to understand that having a distant, condescending, even violent father could make those qualities seem inevitable, even like home. Because of my father, only kind men felt like home.

• • •

Our tactics must always reflect our goals. There is no such thing as killing for peace, strengthening people by making their decisions for them, or suppressing dissent to gain freedom.

We are the women our parents warned us
against—and we are proud!

. . .

Don't wait for others to decide your life—not
a husband, not children, and not convention.
You decide.

. . .

If I had one piece of advice to give to young
girls, I would say, "Don't listen to my advice.
Listen to the voice inside." It's not important
that they know who I am, it's important they
know who they are.

FROM FRIENDS

"Without community, there is no liberation."

AUDRE LORDE

"I am a feminist, and what that means to me is much the same as the meaning of the fact that I am Black: it means that I must undertake to love myself and to respect myself as though my very life depends upon self-love and self-respect."

JUNE JORDAN

"Patriarchy is so universal and normalized that it's like asking a fish *what is water?*"

MONA ELTAHAWY

"First we need a Declaration of Independence, then we need a Declaration of *Interdependence*."

BELLA ABZUG

"The connections between and among women are the most feared, the most problematic, and the most potentially transforming force on the planet."

ADRIENNE RICH

Women may be the only group that grows more radical with age.

CHAPTER 2

Changing Aging

Age should be personal, not political, but we're not quite there yet. There is still an idea that women are valued mostly for reproduction, and men should be older and in authority. That's why youth in women may still be more valued than experience.

We ourselves internalize a life structured by gender. For instance, even though I didn't have the goal of having children, gender still made me feel that I didn't have the power to plan my own future. I was doing what I loved day by day, but it seemed temporary. Even without the demands of husband and family, I was still expecting some mysterious force to take over.

The same is true for making a home, something women are supposed to do for others, not for ourselves. As my friend the photographer Jill Krementz once said after many years of doing work she loved, yet living in a temporary way, "If I'd known life was going to be like this, I would have bought a lamp and a rug."

Female human beings may be more ourselves before we are ten or so, before gender expectations begin to kick in, and perhaps again after we've passed the age of having and raising children. As Carolyn Heilbrun explained so well in *Writing a Woman's Life,* a woman may become a completely different person after fifty. That's because she is at last free to be the grown-up version of the little girl she once was, climbing trees and saying, *I know what I want, I know what I think.* The best indication of who we will be after fifty may be who we were at ten.

This is why there are so many outrageous and brave older women out there. From what I see on the road, they are especially likely to be women of color, perhaps because the dependent feminine role was always less possible, since black men weren't allowed to be as powerful as white men. Whatever the reason and whoever the women, if I could wish any single group into power in the world, it would be these strong, funny, and wise gray-haired women. One day, an army of gray-haired women may quietly take over the earth.

one day, an ARMY of GRAY-HAIRED WOMEN may quietly TAKE OVER THE EARTH.

MOST OF THE PEOPLE I WORK WITH EVERY DAY ARE YOUNGER THAN MY BLUE JEANS!

Now more young women are also questioning the old ways and figuring out how to withstand the tyranny of expectations. Since the women I work with every day are younger than my blue jeans, I experience the pleasure of escaping age segregation, which is as wrong and divisive as any other form of segregation. For instance, because I am older and remember when things were worse, I bring them the gift of hope and optimism. Because they are younger, they see how unjust things still are and have a stake in the future, they bring me the gift of anger and impatience. I can't think of a better combination.

Now that I'm usually the oldest in a group, I found a poem, one of the very few I've ever written, from two decades ago when I was just beginning to discover the blessings of aging:

Dear Goddess: I pray for the courage
To walk naked
At any age.
To wear red and purple,
To be unladylike,
Inappropriate,
Scandalous and
Incorrect
To the very end.

Now all I have to do is live up to my own expectations.

It's hard to understand mortality because inside, being eighty doesn't feel any different from being forty.

• • •

I'm beginning to realize the pleasure of being a nothing-to-lose, take-no-shit older woman.

• • •

I tell everyone in the world my age because I'm trying to believe it myself.

• • •

This is what fifty looks like. We've been lying so long, who would know?

I said those words decades ago, and I just keep saying them. But as I approached my eighties, the word *still* entered my life: "Are you still traveling?" "Are you still writing?" Beware of the *still*s. We are who we always were.

I've always wanted to do a stand-up comedy act, and now I have my first line:

At my age, most people are dead!

I'm at an age when remembering something right away is as good as an orgasm!

. . .

A great thing about aging is that all those brain cells that were once devoted to sex are now available for anything else!

. . .

You're going to make mistakes, and you will learn from them. Say you're sorry, ask what you could have done better, learn—
and move on.

. . .

When people ask me why I still have hope and energy after all these years, I always say: *Because I travel.*

. . .

The things you regret sometimes turn out to be the things you celebrate. In other words: You learn from what you do wrong.

WE DON'T GROW BETTER OR WORSE WITH AGE, JUST MORE LIKE THE UNIQUE SELVES WE WERE BORN TO BE BEFORE MADE-UP GENDER ROLES TOOK OVER OUR CENTRAL YEARS.

If we bless our bodies, our bodies
will bless us.

• • •

When I see the funny, smart, great young
women of today, I think: *I just had to wait for
some of my friends to be born.*

• • •

Imagine your future self walking on the path
ahead of you. Let her lead you.

• • •

Growth comes from saying *yes* to the
unknown.

FROM FRIENDS

"Take a risk—grow old."

ALICE WALKER

"We are all engaged in the task of peeling off the false selves,
the programmed selves, the selves created by our families,
our cultures, our religions."

ANAÏS NIN

"People will forget what you said. People will forget what you
did. But people will never forget how you made them feel."

MAYA ANGELOU

"No black woman writer in this culture can write 'too much.'
Indeed, no woman writer can write 'too much.' . . . No woman
has ever written enough."

BELL HOOKS

"I didn't know what I wanted to do, but I always knew the
woman I wanted to be."

DIANE VON FURSTENBERG

"If you are always trying to be normal, you will never know how amazing you can be."

MAYA ANGELOU

"Feminism is for everybody."

BELL HOOKS

"Sometimes I flip off the 'how I'm supposed to look and be' signs as I fly past them on the way to my chosen dreams."

KATHY NAJIMY

"The purpose of ass-kicking is not that your ass gets kicked at the right time or for the right reason, it's to keep your ass *sensitive.*"

FLO KENNEDY

CHAPTER 3

Work Is Not a
Four-Letter Word

There are few things in life as exciting as discovering we can do something that people value. Remember the first time you mowed the lawn, shoveled snow, or did some other service for a neighbor and were thanked and paid for it?

That's the feeling of working of our own free will, doing something as well as we can, being rewarded for it, and learning by practice how to do it better.

If we could just hang on to these principles for the rest of our lives, we would be a lot happier. To quote Marge Piercy in her great poem "To Be of Use":

The pitcher cries for water to carry
And a person for work that is real.

In the world of rich versus poor, the poor obviously suffer more. Yet the rich may never discover their own talent, or work as its own reward. That's pretty painful. In fact, I would use the pain of work deprivation as an argument against inherited wealth.

If we are lucky enough to find work that we love, we know that we would do it whether or not we got paid. This doesn't mean that we stop fighting for fair and equal wages, but we know we're in the right place when we can't tell the difference between work and life. Yes, we all deserve a cheerful place to live, healthy food, and dancing, but after that, what we do all day should be our greatest pleasure.

Artists and organizers are among those who often have work that is its own reward. As part of the second group, I can tell you how much more satisfying it is than just stockpiling money. When a stranger comes up to me in the street and tells me that something in life is better because of a movement I'm part of, it is way more satisfying than a fancy house or car. Indeed, fancy houses and cars may just isolate us from each other.

I think there should be a course at Harvard Business School that offers a more accurate kind of accounting than just numbers. Such as measuring "Gross National Happiness," which right now only happens in Bhutan. It's a bottom line that includes culture, environment, and governance, yet so far the stock market hasn't noticed.

Whether we work to live, as most of us do, or live to work, as some of us are lucky enough to do, *work* doesn't have to be a four-letter word. It can and should be a source of belonging, growth, and pleasure.

Yet even work we love needs to be acknowledged, and for generations, women who work at home have been called women who don't work. In fact, they perform about a third of all productive work in the United States and many other countries. In less developed parts of the world where women grow much of the food their families eat, this work at home is an even bigger part of the economy. Yet this indispensable work just doesn't show up in the Gross Domestic Product. If it did, $513 billion more would be added to our national economy, and we would have more realistic facts on which to plan.

On top of that, even paid work is often valued more by who does it than by the work itself. For instance, white physicians earn more than black physicians, black female doctors earn less than black male doctors, and female childcare attendants often earn less than male parking lot attendants.

So while we're fighting for better measures of work and how it is rewarded, we can also focus on what work means. When economist John Kenneth Galbraith was trying to evaluate work, he would ask people to list what they learned in each job, and use that as a guide to its value.

By that measure, I would put my teenage jobs right up there with my college degree. When I was working in a women's dress shop after school and on Saturdays, for instance, I learned from listening to grown-up women colleagues about good and bad marriages; how much more they would be earning if local factories hired women; and the Christmas Club that was profiting this dress store chain at the expense of its trusting customers, who were encouraged to make monthly payments toward buying gifts, while the store got the interest.

I also had jobs dancing at conventions and supermarket openings, and that reality got me over my movie-inspired notion that becoming a dancer was a better future than going to college. When I worked as a magician's assistant, and he skipped town with the money he owed me and others, I learned that employees should ask for references from employers, not just the other way around.

My best job for learning was as a swimming instructor and lifeguard at a public city pool over a college summer. As the only white staff member on my shift at this pool in a black neighborhood, I learned from my patient co-workers who just waited for my self-consciousness to go away, then taught me how to play Bones with the kids, and, on rainy days, the card game Bid Whist with the staff. They also showed me how to survive with humor the white teenage boys who shouted racist insults as they raced past on their bikes. When one of my male colleagues yelled back that I was just "a recessive gene," he was rewarded by their confusion. Since those boys made us laugh rather than fear, they finally stopped shouting.

Altogether, I probably learned more useful knowledge in my high school and college jobs than in the classroom.

I suggest that you list all the work you've ever done,

regardless of salary or status, and see what each job taught you. Maybe you will be as unexpectedly grateful as I am.

And once I became a freelance writer and editor, I found the work I really loved. I also discovered the joys of editorial meetings where the staff tried out ideas for articles, names for features, cover lines, and what are known in magazine language as pull quotes or blurbs, a few words in big letters that pull readers into the text.

Like jazz musicians riffing off each other's creativity, we all came up with ideas we might never have imagined on our own.

When Clay Felker started *New York* magazine, the first of all the city magazines, he gathered writers of style and unique voices, from Jimmy Breslin to Tom Wolfe. I was the only "girl writer," though soon there would be more. I realized I had to stay out of the office, except for editorial meetings and delivering articles; otherwise, I would be asked to type and make phone calls.

Since my job was to name all the departments and columns, I gave myself a column called "The City Politic." I had rarely been allowed to write anything political in my freelance career. Soon this allowed me to report on one of the early feminist speak-outs against illegal abortion.

Only three years later, as the women's movement exploded, there was clearly a need for a feminist magazine. A group of women writers and editors started *Ms.*, the first national feminist monthly, and I discovered work that I not only loved but that gave me purpose.

We reported on such once unnamed and invisible realities as *domestic violence, sexual harassment,* and *sex
trafficking,* plus the *double jeopardy* of race and sex discrimination combined, a term invented by writer and activist Frances Beal. Later, law professor Kimberlé
Crenshaw coined *intersectionality* to include the intertwined experiences of race, sex, class, sexual orientation,
age, and more. These realities became more visible and
sharable once there was a term to use.

At *Ms.* we learned and listened, we innovated and ar-
gued, and we made discoveries that changed our own
lives. Editorial meetings became places for feminists
from other countries to drop in and add ideas and diver-
sify experience. Altogether, this was work at its best.

Each week letters from readers poured in by the thousands. From them, we learned about changes long before
they could be measured in public opinion polls. Titles of
books that energized a movement also came to symbolize
it, like *The Feminine Mystique* by Betty Friedan, and *Sisterhood Is Powerful* plus *Sisterhood Is Global,* two land-
mark feminist anthologies created by Robin Morgan. *All
the Women Are White, All the Blacks Are Men, but Some of
Us Are Brave* was a title that captured the lived reality of
black women and became a foundational text of women's
studies. Co-edited by Akasha Gloria Hull, Patricia Bell-
Scott, and Barbara Smith, this anthology took the prize
for the most quoted title.

Now, decades later, Robin Morgan's quotes have become so much a part of global feminism that they are printed on Dior-designed T-shirts and sold to support global feminist activism.

My book titles also started out as quotes. *Moving Beyond Words* was the end of a longer quote that described my time spent on the road as an organizer:

> *I have met brave women who are exploring the outer edge of human possibility, with no history to guide them, and with a courage to make themselves vulnerable that I find moving beyond words.*

Outrageous Acts and Everyday Rebellions came from my organizer's deal that I made—and still make—with audiences at the end of our time together:

> *Promise me that in the next twenty-four hours, you will commit one outrageous act in the cause of justice. It could be as simple as saying, "Pick it up yourself," or as radical as telling each other our salaries. And if you do, I promise you two things: First, the world will be better by the very next day. Second, you will have such a good time that you will never again wake up saying, "Will I do an outrageous act?" Only, "Which outrageous act will I do today?"*

I also encourage people in the audience to introduce themselves to three or four people around them. After all, if we came to this event, we probably share interests and values, so just say what you care about, why you came, what work you do, or what you hope for. Then each of us may leave with a new job, a new colleague, a new revolutionary idea, a new love affair—who knows what might happen?

Over the years, I've discovered countless stories of what came from this simple permission. One recent surprise came in a letter from a ninety-year-old retired physician:

> *I turned to my left and introduced myself to a Mrs. Barbara Drench, longstanding philanthropist and involved in numerous international and national U.S./Israeli organizations. I gave her my name, and she returned with her name, and at the same time, we each said, I have heard your name before when dear friends tried to introduce us.*
>
> *Gloria, the rest is history. We soon started dating, and are now involved deeply in a wonderful and exciting and loving and caring relationship. Both of us are widowers and had deeply loving marriages. When asked, how did we meet, we always say, Gloria Steinem introduced us.*

This is just one of endless proofs that we may never know what will come of our work. The only lasting guide is: Do work you love.

Don't worry about what you should do, just do whatever you can.

Women are always saying, "We can do anything that men can do." But men are not saying, "We can do anything that women can do."

• • •

No man can call himself liberal, or radical, or even a conservative advocate of fair play if his work depends in any way on the unpaid or underpaid labor of women at home or in the workplace.

• • •

The first problem for all of us, men and women, is not to learn but to unlearn.

There are black doctors and doctors and
women novelists and novelists.
Any less powerful group gets the adjective,
while the powerful group takes the noun.
The less powerful group usually knows the
more powerful one much better than vice
versa. People of color have to understand
white people in order to survive; women
have had to know men. Only the powerful
group can afford to regard the less
powerful one as a mystery.

MEN ARE LIKED
BETTER WHEN THEY WIN.
WOMEN ARE LIKED
BETTER WHEN
THEY LOSE.

MEN | WOMEN

This is how
the patriarchy is
enforced everyday.

There are really not many jobs that actually require a penis or a vagina, and all other occupations should be open to everyone.

• • •

The gender ghetto in journalism was not just a glass ceiling, it was a glass box.

• • •

Prostitution isn't the oldest profession, it's the oldest oppression.

Once, sexual harassment was just called life.

• • •

Once, domestic violence was just called life.

We could insert many words in here, all thanks to the women's movement, which invented terms to make the invisible visible. For something to become distinct, it has to have a name. As Susanne K. Langer, the great American philosopher, said, "The notion of giving something a name is the vastest generative idea that was ever conceived." No wonder patriarchal marriage took women's names away, and egalitarian marriage is giving them back. And no wonder you may not know Susanne Langer. It's because her name wasn't Stephen or Samuel. Look her up.

Once upon a time, a "liberated woman" was only somebody who had sex before marriage and a job afterward. I call that a reform, not a revolution.

. . .

The truth is that every country has its own organic feminism. Far more than communism, capitalism, or any other philosophy I can think of, it is a grassroots event. It grows in women's heads and hearts.

. . .

A gender-equal society would be one where the word *gender* does not exist, where everyone can be a unique self.

People before paper; stories before statistics.

• • •

People who are experiencing a problem are
the most likely to know its solution.

• • •

The media are not reality; reality is reality.

In this wired world that allows a half-existence of faraway
voices and images, yet rarely a full life of being a hundred
percent where we actually are, it's time to state the obvious:
The media are not reality. Reality is reality. We can empathize only when we are together with all five senses.

DON'T CHANGE WOMEN TO
FIT THE WORLD; CHANGE THE
WORLD TO FIT WOMEN.

You can tell what your values are by looking at how you spend your extra money.

. . .

Planning ahead is a measure of class. Rich people can plan for generations ahead. Poor people plan for Saturday night.

. . .

Try not to generalize. Even rich white guys are not all alike. Warren Buffett is not a Koch brother.

. . .

America is an enormous frosted cupcake in the middle of millions of starving people.

FEEL THE

FEAR —

AND DO IT

ANYWAY.

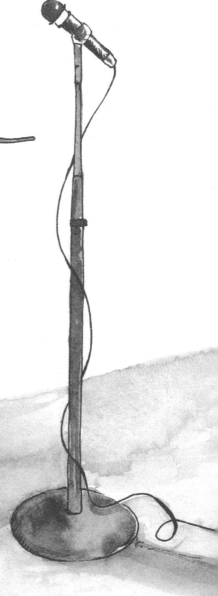

All movements need a few people who can't be fired. If you're dependent, it's very hard not to be concerned about the approval of whoever and whatever you're dependent on.

• • •

While I was traveling as an organizer, I discovered that ordinary people are smart, smart people are ordinary, decisions are best made by the people affected by them, and human beings have an almost infinite capacity for adapting to the expectations around us.

The only thing worse than failing is not having tried. You will walk around forever thinking, *What if?*

. . .

Being brave is not being unafraid, but feeling the fear and doing it anyway.

. . .

Fear is a sign of growth.

The art of life is not controlling what happens,
it's using what happens.

• • •

If you find yourself drawn to an event against
all logic, go. The universe is telling you
something.

• • •

Limits lead to invention.

FROM FRIENDS

"I am myself—a Black woman warrior poet doing my work—
come to ask you, are you doing yours?"

AUDRE LORDE

"I was raised to believe that excellence is the best deterrent to
racism and sexism. And that's how I operate my life."

OPRAH WINFREY

"Talent is really enjoying something long enough to get good
at it."

NELL PAINTER

"The function, the very serious function of racism, is
distraction."

TONI MORRISON

"My grandfather once told me that there were two kinds of
people—those who do the work and those who take the
credit. He told me to try to be in the first group; there was
much less competition."

INDIRA GANDHI

"Sexual harassment turns real work into an arm of the sex trade. The imperative to exchange sex for survival, or the dangled possibility of survival whether real or not, governs women's inequality, hence women's lives, worldwide."

CATHARINE MACKINNON

we learn from
DIFFERENCE,
not from sameness.

CHAPTER 4

Among Co-conspirators and Adversaries

I'm not sure we can predict our feeling of being drawn to some people and not to others, of feeling seen by them or not, but I am sure we know it when we feel it.

When I was a child, a couple of high school girls looked after me while my parents were working at the summer resort that was our family business. One did everything she was supposed to do. The other waited until my parents were gone, then went off dancing with her boyfriend.

I tolerated the first, but I loved the second. Why? Because before she climbed out the window and into the summer night, she asked me which earrings to wear and if I liked her perfume. The first treated me like an interchangeable child. The second asked my opinion. Nothing, but nothing, replaces the feeling of being seen and valued.

A few years ago, I was at a conference where the singer and songwriter Naomi Judd was speaking about women's health. She had been supporting a Republican presidential candidate, and I was supporting a Democratic one, yet she sought me out and said she hoped I would meet her daughter because we had so much in common.

I did have lunch with her daughter, Ashley Judd, and we've been friends and co-conspirators ever since. She is not only a magical actor but travels the world to support work against sex trafficking and other violence against women.

We also campaign for the same candidates at home. Her mother may still prefer the opposition, but she isn't an adversary because she respects and allows differences. This is all the more important today when we have world leaders who don't respect difference. That lack of respect is dictatorship.

Sometimes showing respect for individuality takes only a second. Last week in an airport, a place I so often am, I noticed that the clerk who was helping me didn't ask me if I wanted a wheelchair, as I guess age guidelines required her to do. She just smiled and said she could see I didn't need one. On my return, another airline clerk looked only at her computer and so ordered a wheelchair, complete with attendant, that might have been needed somewhere else. To one, I was an individual human being. To the other, I was a group.

I give these small examples to say that the distinction between an adversary and a co-conspirator isn't always determined by issues and beliefs. The more crucial distinction is that adversaries ignore or condemn your difference from them, while co-conspirators either agree with you or allow you to be who you are.

Of course, the need to wipe out difference doesn't come from nothing—that person probably has been ignored and wiped out themselves—but it's still part of the problem.

Movements are mostly made up of people who agree on what should be done and who listen to each other's different ideas about how to do it. Yet sometimes people who agree on goals and should be co-conspirators turn into adversaries. This can be especially painful.

I'm not talking about a spirited argument or debate, but a need to negate the presence and stop the ascent of another person by questioning their motive, judging their group, falsifying their character, and essentially invalidating them.

If this sounds familiar in your experience or observation, read the classic essay "Trashing," by Jo Freeman, a political scientist, feminist activist, and very wise woman. She wrote this essay in the early days of feminism, and what you are experiencing now may not be as painful as what she describes. There were way more wounded people then, and way less healing to go around. Some activists who had been robbed of individuality as women punished individuality among feminists.

Now, there is a lot more understanding that success is not a zero-sum game, and that we need and benefit from each other's examples of success in all our diversity. Yes, trashing and trolling on the Internet are still painful parallels to the past, and now they travel so fast that they can seem unbearable. But at least now this pain is a recognized and condemned phenomenon, not a singular and deserved fate.

The medium and degree may have changed, but the intent and hurt may be the same. If we have internalized the hierarchies imposed on us, we may still see success as a zero-sum game.

In the early years of the women's movement, for instance, an older woman identified with the movement first welcomed me as a supporter. Then she criticized me and also a couple of other women who got elected to political office or otherwise became publicly identified with feminism. I hadn't changed, and neither had they, but we were being recognized, and the older woman leader felt threatened by that.

In reality, what this leader had done was unique and could never be replaced or challenged, yet she seemed to believe that recognition is a zero-sum game. She also had opinions that came from her generation and experience, and she lashed out when others didn't accept those opinions. For instance, she feared that a focus on discrimination against lesbians or on the plight of welfare mothers would make the feminist movement unacceptable in the powerful places it needed to go. I thought we should be unified, even if it made progress slower, and dividing ourselves was a form of self-defeat.

Gradually, I noticed that when others disagreed with

her in exactly the same way I did, she did not attack them the way she attacked me. She also was unwilling to explore what we could do together. Instead, she condemned me in public, even though I didn't respond.

For many years, this behavior continued to be mystifying and very painful. Though one-sided, the media reported it as a catfight and proof that women were each other's worst enemies.

Years later, her younger sister, a woman I had never met, wrote me a letter. She started by saying that she had found that painful events become less painful once their cause is understood, so she wanted to explain what she thought was triggering her older sister's behavior. Throughout their growing-up and student years, she had been regarded as the beautiful one, and this had blighted her older sister's life. No matter how much the younger one tried to make up for this unfairness, it remained a bitter reality. Also, this younger sister had chosen and was happy in a traditional marriage, and she believed this was why her older sister focused on criticizing such marriages in her writing.

The point of her letter to me was this: She wanted me to know that I had come to represent her, in her sister's mind. She hoped my understanding this would give me some comfort, and tell me that fixing it was not in my control.

It definitely did both. I've always been grateful.

We can't always know what bruise from the past is

making a current touch painful. We can only do our best, as this younger sister did, to understand in the present. She helped me to do that too.

Of course, the above example of repeating a past trauma is rare. Most people who share goals do become co-conspirators, listen to each other, respond as individuals, and honor whoever we uniquely are.

Yet some adversaries are still insecure without a hierarchy, whether in big categories like gender, race, class, and religion or in personal biases about education or how we look. Labels are created by culture, not by nature. The problem is not only the idea that one group should be on top, but also the idea that there is a top at all. As I write this, about a third of my own country, the United States, is in full backlash against the loss of an old hierarchy, and, due to an anomaly of our electoral system, has managed to elect a president who promises a return to the past.

In fact, if you go back to most of human history, not just what we probably studied as history, our primordial form was not a hierarchy but a circle. If our study of history began with the time when people started, not when patriarchy, colonialism, and racism started, we might have a very different idea of what is possible.

Fortunately, human beings come equipped with empathy, otherwise our species could not survive. If we see another person hurt or suffering—and are present with all five senses, not just surfing the Internet—we are flooded with oxytocin, the tend-and-befriend hormone. Whether we are male or female, oxytocin rises in us when we hold a baby, or when we see another human being in an accident and rush to help. And oxytocin is also often the key to turning an adversary into a co-conspirator. If you listen, truly listen, to an adversary, you will probably find at least one goal on which you agree. And even if you don't, you will reduce the hostility level by your openness to and honoring of your adversary's views.

People in the same room can understand and empathize with each other in a way that isn't possible on the page or screen. I'm happy you are reading this book, but I hope you will also put the book down and spend at least as much time talking and listening to the stories of other human beings. We need to be together to empathize, and our minds are organized by narrative. We haven't been telling our stories around campfires for hundreds of thousands of years for nothing.

As I travel, I notice that even children everywhere seem to say in some form, "You are not the boss of me." Does that sound familiar? It's because we're born feeling unique and connected, seeking the expressions of others but also expressing ourselves. There is already a person inside every baby.

True adversaries treat us as if we were blank slates on which they could write anything, categorizing us by race, gender, or current need. They may be dictators or just people who don't listen, but they impose the tyranny of their own agendas and expectations.

Movements are groups of people who once had such views of others imposed on them and are now trying to become the unique people they were born to be. In many ways, "race" is an invention of colonialism. It rationalized the taking over of other people's countries, even the crime of slavery.

Co-conspirators may be family members or a chosen family of friends, a work cohort, a movement, or all of the above, but they listen as much as they talk, they talk as much as they listen, and they help each other become who they were born to be.

And remember that having some adversaries is a good thing. If these individual or collective dictators were on your side, you would know you were doing something wrong.

THE WORLD IS DIVIDED
INTO TWO KINDS OF PEOPLE.

THOSE WHO DIVIDE
EVERYTHING
INTO TWO,

AND THOSE WHO DON'T.

Feminism starts out being the instinct of the little child who says, "It's not fair." It ends up being a worldview that questions hierarchy altogether.

• • •

Only when the bottom moves does the whole hierarchy topple.

• • •

A pedestal is as much a prison as any other small space.

(This was said to be a warning by black suffragists to white wives of plantation owners in the South.)

Sometimes life is like trying to paint the Sistine Chapel ceiling on the backs of five thousand turtles.

• • •

No wonder studies show that women's intellectual self-esteem tends to go down with every year of higher education. We've been studying our own absence.

• • •

Being misunderstood by people whose opinions you value is way more painful than being condemned by your enemies.

We have to behave
as though everything
we do matters —
because it might.

Shared purpose eliminates hierarchy.

• • •

Every woman knows there is a big difference
between help that is designed to keep you
dependent, and help that is designed to make
you independent.

ELEPHANTS ARE NON VIOLENT, THEY'RE MATRILINEAL, VEGETARIAN, THEY HAVE A SENSE OF HUMOR, LONG MEMORIES~ If only we could all be a little more like elephants.

Not one study has proved that women talk more than men, but numerous studies indicate that men talk more than women. Women are thought to be more talkative than men because they are being measured against the expectation of female silence.

• • •

Audiences turn into partners if you just listen to them as much as you talk.

• • •

We don't learn while we're talking, we learn while we're listening.

Categories are the
enemy of connection.

• • •

Empathy is the most radical of human
emotions.

• • •

Ceremony is something that is always the
same and is dictated from above. Ritual is
something that uses universal human symbols
and changes with every group.

If you want people to listen to you, you have to listen to them.

. . .

I've come to have great faith in the magic of people talking together after a shared experience.

. . .

Talking circles remind us that simple things are useful, useful things are simple, and being together with other human beings is as necessary as air, food, and water.

. . .

In a circle, we are looking *at* each other, not *up* or *down*.

The first resistance to social change is to say:
It's not necessary.

• • •

A true adversary is probably somebody
with a big empathy deficit.

There is no virtue
in being on the same page
if it's the wrong page.

If you tell me a statistic, I'll make up a story to explain why it's true. Our brains are organized by narrative and image, not facts and numbers.

• • •

It is truly amazing how long we can go on accepting myths that oppose our own lives.

• • •

Oral history turns out to be more accurate than written history because the experiences of generations on the ground are way more accurate than a few guys generalizing from above.

Beware of any motto that glorifies the past. It's code for restoring hierarchy. For example: "Make America great again."

• • •

I once heard a great quote in the National Museum of the American Indian, and I always pass it on: "There are two things, history and the past—and they are not the same."

• • •

What we know as "history" is not history. Put another way: "It's called 'history' because it is his story."

Women have always been an equal part of the past, JUST NOT AN EQUAL PART OF HISTORY.

We are communal animals. There is a reason why solitary confinement counts as torture.

• • •

Technology is a gift and a blessing— providing you spend as much time with human beings as you do with screens.

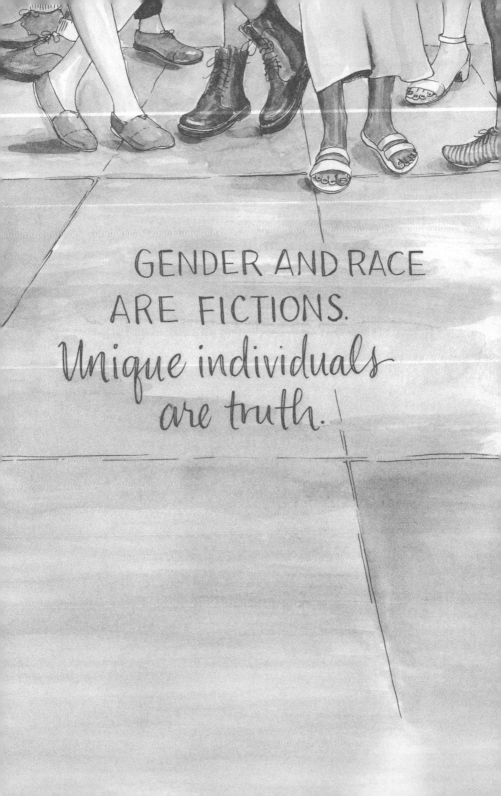

GENDER AND RACE
ARE FICTIONS.
Unique individuals
are truth.

People invented race and gender. People can uninvent them.

• • •

For every purpose other than reproduction on the one hand and resistance to certain diseases on the other, the differences between individuals of the same sex or race are much greater than those between males and females or between races as groups.

• • •

Original languages didn't have gender— people were people. So how did we get so crazy as to give gender to tables and chairs?

• • •

The marks of sex and race bring a whole constellation of cultural injunctions against power, even the power of controlling one's own life.

Racism is white people's problem. Violence against women is men's problem.

. . .

White parents should pay to have their children bused into schools that look like the country. Otherwise their children will grow up thinking that everybody looks and lives like them.

. . .

Racist systems must control wombs and the bodies of women in order to keep races separate. To end racism is to free all women—and vice versa.

I began to joke about putting this sign on the road to Harvard, Yale, and Princeton after I encountered everyday women who said one of the saddest sentences on earth: "I'm not smart enough to be a feminist." Academic language didn't welcome them. This broke my heart. Women's Studies came from women's lived lives and was meant to be just the beginning. Women in all our diversity should be half of history, literature, Black Studies, science, everything. Words that need explaining make academia seem isolated and only for the few.

And if you think I'm kidding, here is the dictionary definition of deconstruction: "a philosophical or critical method which asserts that meanings, metaphysical constructs, and hierarchical oppositions (as between key terms in philosophical or literary work) are always rendered unstable by their dependence on ultimately arbitrary signifiers." I rest my case.

One of the most radical things we can be is understandable, which is why I love quotes. Women's Studies are really Remedial Studies, and should be available to everyone.

Needing approval is a female cultural disease
and so it is often a sign that we are doing the
wrong thing.

• • •

There is still no "right" way to be a woman
in public power without being considered
a you-know-what.

Said another way:

A woman who aspires to be something
will be called a bitch.

• • •

Anything that affects males is often seen as
more serious than anything that affects "only"
the female half of the human race.

If they call you a bitch, Say:

THANK YOU!

If someone called me a lesbian, I said, "Thank you." It disclosed nothing, confused the accuser, conveyed solidarity with women who are lesbians, and made the audience laugh.

Power CAN BE TAKEN,
NOT GIVEN.

ONLY TAKING Power
GIVES YOU THE STRENGTH
TO USE IT.

Power DOESN'T HAVE
TO BE Power OVER,
IT CAN BE power TO DO.

IT'S EASIER TO BLAME
THE PERSON WITH
LESS Power.

An obsession with approval in the present, feminine-style, or with controlling and living in the future, masculine-style, are both wasteful of time. And time is all there is.

• • •

Women are required to be strong, then are punished for our strength.

EVIL is OBVIOUS

OBVIOUS

ONLY IN RETROSPECT

When feminism got to the point of serious opposition, it was a step forward from ridicule.

• • •

Whether we conform to it or fight it, the *it* is still the problem.

• • •

If women are supposed to be less rational and more emotional at the beginning of our menstrual cycle, when the female hormone is at its lowest level, then why isn't it logical to say that, in those few days, women behave the most like the way men behave all month long?

Trust Your Intuition—
IF IT WALKS LIKE A Duck,
AND QUACKS LIKE A Duck, BUT YOU
THINK IT'S A
Pig—
IT'S A Pig!

God may be in the details, but the Goddess is in the connections.

• • •

Nothing is more dangerous than someone who believes that life after death is better than life. Doomsday religions are now coinciding with doomsday weapons.

• • •

Why does God always look like the ruling class? Why is Jesus pictured as blond and blue-eyed in the Middle East? Because if God is a white man, a white man is God.

• • •

It's an incredible con job when you think about it: Patriarchal religions get us to believe and behave now for a reward after death. Even corporations only promise to reward you after retirement.

PERFECT IS BORING;
beauty is irregular.

Whatever you do with the way you look, try not to let it distract from what you're saying.

. . .

It's said that the biggest determinant of our lives is whether we see the world as welcoming or hostile. This becomes a self-fulfilling prophecy.

. . .

A quail is just a chicken with a press agent.

FROM FRIENDS

"It is not our differences that divide us, it is our Inability to recognize, accept, and celebrate those differences."

AUDRE LORDE

"When men are oppressed, it's tragedy. When women are oppressed, it's tradition."

BERNADETTE MOSALA

"Any God I ever felt in church I brought with me."

ALICE WALKER

"Make your heart too rebellious for patriarchy to plant itself within you. Make your mind too free for fascism to claim your imagination."

MONA ELTAHAWY

"Sometimes people try to destroy you, precisely because they recognize your power—not because they don't see it, but because they see it and don't want it to exist."

BELL HOOKS

"Hate generalizes, love specifies."

ROBIN MORGAN

"The root of oppression is the loss of memory."

PAULA GUNN ALLEN

CHAPTER 5

Laughing Our Way to the Revolution

Laughter is the only free emotion. It is the essence of humanity and free will, an orgasm of the mind. If you think this is overstating the importance of laughter, here is a fact: Laughter is the only emotion that cannot be compelled.

We can be forced to fear, and a good thing too, because it's part of the reason our species survives. We can be compelled to love, because if someone is dependent for long enough, love of self and love of another become intertwined by our instinct for survival. This may mean captives loving their captors, as in the Stockholm syndrome, but the point is that this, too, is a response to the will to survive.

But laughter! Ah, laughter has no tactical purpose. It can't be compelled. It is the ultimate proof of our humanity. It just explodes from within like a great *aha!*

Laughter arrives when two opposites collide and suddenly create a third, when we have a flash of understanding, when a punch line changes everything that has gone before, when we glimpse a new possibility. Albert Einstein once famously said that he had to be very careful while shaving because if he had a new idea, he laughed and cut himself.

Laughter is the most contagious of all emotions. Our pulse and blood pressure go up. We breathe faster and send more oxygen to our brains. A doctor found that a minute of laughter stimulated his heart as much as ten minutes of rowing. It's a full-on collaboration between mind and body.

Because the power to say things that create laughter really *is* a power, women are not supposed to have it. Female comics are relatively rare and new. This may also be because studies show that what women fear most in men is violence, but what men fear most in women is ridicule.

In a political candidate, we should look for an ability to laugh, especially at oneself. I bet there is an inverse relationship between authoritarianism and a sense of humor.

Any single one of these benefits would be enough to make us value laughter, but the big one is this: Laughter is a proof of freedom. No one, but no one, can *force* us to laugh. When we experience this orgasm of the mind, we are truly free.

So use laughter as a guide:

- Try to stay away from places where you're not allowed to laugh, including religious ones. The absence of laughter is a giveaway that the religion in question is more political than spiritual, more about a hierarchy with God at the top than about godliness in all living things.

- Try to stay away from workplaces where laughter is absent. The degree of freedom where you work is indicated by the presence or absence of laughter.
- Try to stay away from social settings with no laughter. Your ability to laugh is a sign that you're doing the right thing with the right people in the right place. Laughing together creates instant community.

Whatever makes us laugh is a good thing, from elaborate jokes to stand-up comedy, but I have a special fondness for spontaneous, in-the-moment laughter.

This is an old tradition in Native American culture, where laughter is personified by the Trickster, a male or female or male-and-female spirit who may turn up anywhere. Unlike the Court Jester or the Circus Clown, who makes the powerful laugh, the Trickster is free, a paradox, a crosser of boundaries who breaks into sacred space and lets laughter out.

Since one Indian Country belief is that sacred space can be pierced only by laughter and prayer, there is also a belief that if we can't laugh, we can't pray. Laughter is the ultimate in you-have-to-be-there.

I hope you will let laughter be your guide to freedom.

Had enough of Trumpian tweets? Remember, the past tense of *tweet* is *twat*!

. . .

The art form of saying *fuck* is to put it in the middle of a word, as in: *Fan-fucking-tastic!*

. . .

Some men inspire poetry:

Each time he said,
"I love you,"
He said, "but I'll get over it,"
And so
I did.

. . .

If movies about relationships are called "chick flicks," why aren't movies about violence called "prick flicks"?

Like Sky Masterson, the wandering gambler in Damon Runyon stories, I've been in more hotel rooms than the Gideon Bible—and he didn't wash his hair with hotel soap, eat from vending machines, or sit up late organizing with the hotel maids.

I'VE BEEN IN MORE HOTEL ROOMS THAN THE GIDEON BIBLE.

MOTEL

It's probably only me, but . . .
I don't know if this is right, but . . .

Never preface what you say with either of those two phrases.
It's a way women disqualify what we know.

• • •

Often asked why you're not married?
Explain: I can't mate in captivity!

• • •

Whatever you want to do, just do it. Making a
damn fool of yourself is absolutely essential.

Never ever
give up...
AND DANCE
A LITTLE!

FROM FRIENDS

"A woman needs a man like a fish needs a bicycle."

IRINA DUNN

In the 1970s I heard this quote, laughed, and repeated it. Then because it was wrongly attributed to me, I began to use any available interview to ask who said it.

Finally in 1994, I did an interview with the Australian Broadcasting Corporation that actually reached the ears of its originator, Irina Dunn, and she wrote me a letter.

She explained that in 1970, she had been reading a philosophy book, whose author she didn't recall, and this sentence caught her attention: "A man needs god like a fish needs a bicycle."

Under the influence of feminism, she changed it to: "A woman needs a man like a fish needs a bicycle." She wrote these words on the wall of two women's restrooms at the University of Sydney, where she was a student. From there, they spread like wildfire.

I tried to find the originator of the quote that had captured her attention in the first place. The best I could come up with was Charles S. Harris, an American psychologist, who wrote in 1958, "A man needs faith like a fish needs a bicycle."

But more important, this search had earned me a wonderful letter from Irina Dunn herself. I learned she was involved in publishing, politics, and the environmental and feminist movements. She even had been elected as a senator from New South Wales.

I still have her letter pinned to my bulletin board. I hope to meet her one day.

Such is the power of a quote heard round the world.

"For a man to be called ruthless, he has to take over your job or your life. For a woman to be called ruthless, she has only to put you on hold."

MARLO THOMAS

"Feminism should terrify the patriarchy."

MONA ELTAHAWY

"Laughter is carbonated holiness."

ANNE LAMOTT

"If men could get pregnant, abortion would be a sacrament."

WOMAN TAXI DRIVER, QUOTED BY FLO KENNEDY
AND GLORIA STEINEM

Flo Kennedy and I were riding in a taxi in Boston talking about Flo's book *Abortion Rap* when the cabbie, an old Irish woman who must have been a rarity in this job, turned around and uttered those memorable words. They have spread to posters and banners, even in street demonstrations outside the Vatican. If you don't know Flo and her words, you are missing out. We once ran a section in *Ms.* called "The Verbal Karate of Florynce R. Kennedy, Esq." Here's a small sampling:

"Trying to help an oppressed person is like trying to put your arm around somebody with a sunburn."

"Don't agonize, organize!"

"Unity in a Movement situation can be overrated. If you were the Establishment, which would you rather see coming in the door: one lion or five hundred mice?"

"The truly fearless think of themselves as normal."

MARGARET ATWOOD

"All the women I know feel a little like outlaws."

MARILYN FRENCH

We don't know
what will
happen, but we
know what
we can do.

CHAPTER 6

In the Street

If you've ever been in a street demonstration or on a picket line, I bet you remember your first time. There is something transgressive about breaking through the anonymity of city streets and daring to care in public.

My first time on a picket line was outside a Manhattan supermarket, asking people to refuse to buy grapes picked in poverty. Unlike the other picketers, I was clearly not a farmworker, and I felt like an idiot.

Then Dolores Huerta, a former farmworker herself and the chief negotiator for the United Farm Workers, dropped by to encourage us. Within minutes, she turned the sidewalk into a stage and caused passersby to stop, listen, cheer, argue, and care. I learned from her that street activism is an art form. You have to look at each person, call out a fragment of a story that makes them want to know more, and just keep going.

You also need a unifying slogan. Ours was *"Sí se puede!"* Yes, we can! Those were the words of migrant farmworkers who had been told for generations that agribusiness was too powerful to defeat, and also left out of legislation that protected other workers. Now they were appealing to a third force: customers who could refuse to buy grapes and other produce harvested in poverty.

It would take five years of this picketing and protesting, but those street demonstrations did have an impact. Agribusiness leaders finally sat down at the negotiating table with farmworkers. Dolores started meetings with a round of *"Sí se puede!"* Yes, we can! She was saying that former adversaries could agree, and also reminding growers of the forces that had driven them to the table in the first place.

Decades later, "Yes, we can!" became the motto of Barack Obama's campaign for the presidency of the United States. Once he became the first African American ever to be elected, thousands gathered in the streets around the Capitol in Washington, a building that had been largely constructed by slaves, shouting those words.

"Yes, we can!" is now part of the language.

Other street quotes are "Make Love, Not War"; "Black Is Beautiful"; "Women's Rights Are Human Rights"; "Immigrants Make America Great"; "Black Lives Matter"; and "Love Is Love," an answer to the idea that marriage is only about reproduction and thus only for a male and female. Now, as an alternative to prostitution and pornography, there is also: "Eroticize Equality."

This street quote actually was made into a T-shirt. *Erotica* is a word that can differentiate sex from violence

and rescue mutual sexual pleasure. It comes from the Greek root *eros,* meaning "love," and has no gender. *Pornography* comes from *porne,* meaning "female sex slave." They are as different as a room with doors open and a room with doors locked. Until we finally separate sexuality from aggression, there will be way more pornography than erotica.

Sometimes street quotes seem to have no author, as if they came from our collective unconscious. After the terrorist attack of 9/11, for instance, a contagious quote was "Our Grief Is Not a Cry for War!" I saw it as graffiti on fences, walls, and sidewalks, often with flowers or photos to honor people who lost their lives.

Later, performance artists carried posters with this quote, standing silently in the street to mark 9/11 anniversaries. Now when visitors pay tribute to 9/11, they may see these words engraved on permanent memorials. Yet no one seems to know for sure where they came from.

Sometimes knowing the source of a quote adds to its meaning. For instance, Alicia Garza, Patrisse Cullors, and Opal Tometi, the three young black feminists who started Black Lives Matter, created three organizing guidelines you may hear, or see scrawled on placards and walls:

1. Lead with love.
2. Low ego, high impact.
3. Move at the speed of trust.

I feel especially good about the future because all three of these women are about half my age, and they have created the best organizing guidelines I've ever heard.

As you find or make up quotes suitable for instant understanding in the street, you may get hooked on writing and discovering more. Words can travel through crowds at the speed of sound, unify disparate people, and encourage us to act together. In the 1960s, when resisting the draft and the Vietnam War could mean you got a fine, prison, or both, crowds of young men began to chant, "Hell no, I won't go!" You could almost hear the power balance shifting.

Once in Chicago, during a Democratic convention where Vietnam was the big issue, I watched as mounted policemen rode into a crowd of several thousand peaceful demonstrators. Like other bystanders, I was sure there would be violence. But people stood their ground and began to chant, "The streets belong to us!" As this chant spread like waves in an ocean, the mounted police slowed and stopped. The last thing I saw was a policeman looking mystified as his horse was being fed an apple by a demonstrator. Those chanted words seemed to change the molecules in the air.

This is why you may get hooked on organizing as street theater. There is something to love about breaking through routine and anonymity, and sharing hope.

Now that we have the Internet, we have faster ways to get words out there, and to give street quotes another life online. Think of the flash mob phenomenon of strangers who meet to dance, sing, perform, or just move in a pattern together—and then disperse. Thanks to the Internet, that can become the joy of flash activism.

Our presence as women in the street, talking, chanting, singing, is evidence of change in itself. Many women still think twice before entering a public space. Crowds present one kind of danger, and empty streets another. For decades, women have demonstrated against sexual assault by using slogans like "Take back the streets" and "Take back the night." Every survey about violence and sexual assault continues to show that women report at least three times more fear of violence than do males. Also in some parts of the world, women are still not allowed to leave their homes, cities, or nations without the presence or written permission of a male relative or guardian. This is an irony because, statistically speaking, women are most likely to be beaten, assaulted, or killed by men they know.

Rather than spend time debating relative dangers, let's just focus on being safer everywhere. It is clear that women are safest in the presence or proximity of other women. Then we can add men we trust.

Consider the famous Women's March of 2017, the one that followed the not-by-popular-vote election of Donald Trump as president. There were so many people in Washington, D.C., that there was no room to march. On the same day, there were also Women's Marches in more than four hundred cities and towns across this country. It was the largest single-day protest in the history of the United States. And there were Women's Marches of support in eighty-one countries on all seven continents.

Yet in all these marches—in this country and as far as is known, around the world—there was not one reported case of violence.

Now that we know how to take back the streets, words and votes are following.

DON'T HOLD A FINGER
TO THE WIND.

BECOME THE WIND.

A movement is only composed of people moving. Feeling its warmth and motion around us is the end as well as the means.

. . .

It's all about freedom. A room with the door locked is a prison, but the very same room with the door open is a home. It's our job to unlock that door.

. . .

The job of a movement is to make what's bad good.

A MOVEMENT IS
LIKE A RIVER,
IT FLOWS IN THE
SAME DIRECTION,
YET IS NEVER
THE SAME TWICE.

Sometimes,

PRESSING SEND ISN'T ENOUGH.

It's great that we can find information and each other on-line, but pressing Send doesn't actually do anything. The Internet is a great gift, perhaps especially to women who can access information and each other in physical safety, yet it can't replace being together with all five senses. Because too many people have been spending more time look-ing at the screen than being together, sadness, isolation, depression, and even suicide are increasing, especially among young people. For every hour we spend on a com-puter or a cellphone, we need an hour with other human beings.

Hope is a form of planning.

Americans seem to outstrip every nation when it comes to hope. Perhaps that's because so many of us came in flight from something worse, or escaped something worse here, or absorbed the fact and fiction of the "land of opportunity," or maybe it's because optimism is contagious. Whatever the reason, hopefulness is what I miss the most when I'm not here. It's the thing that makes me glad to come home. I often describe myself as a "hope-a-holic."

Feminism has a history. It is the keystone of any organic and lasting democracy.

. . .

The Constitution does not begin with "I, the president." It begins with "We, the people."

. . .

What did Columbus call primitive?
Equal women!

Our Constitution is based on the Iroquois Confederacy, which is the oldest continuous democracy on earth. It was a real democracy in which women and men were valued equally. For instance, the chief might have been male, but he was chosen by female elders. Because of this history, Benjamin Franklin invited male leaders from the Confederacy to advise on structuring the Constitution. It is said that their first question was "Where are the women?"

I'VE SEEN ENOUGH CHANGE TO KNOW THAT MORE WILL COME.

When anybody asks me, "What should I do?"
I say, "Just do whatever you can."

• • •

There is no such thing as working "outside
the system." It's just a question of working
where you can be most effective.

• • •

When unique voices are united in a common
cause, they make history.

Every movement has come from people
sharing their stories.

. . .

The women's movement often came out of
talking circles that were called
consciousness-raising groups, just as the civil
rights movement often came out of groups in
black churches in the South testifying and
saying, "Here's what happened to me,"
and other people saying, "That happened
to me too." We discover we are not
crazy and we are not alone.

. . .

The women's movement and the civil rights
movement and the Chinese Revolution
started with talking circles.

The source of every social justice movement is people sitting in circles saying the unsayable thing—and discovering it's happened to other people, too. If you come together, you can change it.

• • •

It was Cesar Chavez and Dolores Huerta who reminded me of what I learned in India: The clearest view is always from the bottom.

• • •

There is no greater gift than thinking you have some impact on the world for the better.

• • •

The future depends entirely on what each of us does every day.

• • •

Sometimes we must put our bodies where our beliefs are.

We're not only having a revolution, but an evolution.

• • •

Like art, revolutions come from combining what exists with what has never existed before.

• • •

You can travel without traveling, and you can *not* travel—yet travel. Being on the road is a state of mind.

Feminism includes all human beings who call ourselves women—or it's not feminism.

. . .

Feminism has never been about getting a job for one woman. It's about making life more fair for women everywhere. It's not about one woman getting a piece of the existing pie; there are too many of us for that. It's about baking a new pie.

. . .

If I could have one wish for the women's movement internationally, it would be a kind of Alcoholics Anonymous structure. Imagine a whole network of little groups meeting in church basements and school gyms and around the well in villages. . . . They're leaderless, and they're free. They have as their goal supporting each other's self-authority.

A FEMINIST IS ANYONE
WHO RECOGNIZES THE
EQUALITY AND HUMANITY
OF ALL PEOPLE.

For women, the only alternative to being a feminist is being a masochist.

• • •

The ends don't justify the means—the means we use dictate the end we get.

• • •

If everyone has a full circle of human qualities to complete, progress lies in the direction we haven't been. It's progress for men to develop so-called feminine qualities and for women to develop so-called masculine qualities. We are all becoming full human beings.

• • •

Law and justice are not always the same. When they aren't, disobeying the law may be the first step toward justice.

Going on the road is right up there with life-threatening emergencies and truly mutual sex as a way of being fully alive in the present.

• • •

The idea of freedom is contagious.

there is
always one
true inner voice:

TRUST
IT.

FROM FRIENDS

"If any female feels she needs anything beyond herself to
legitimate and validate her existence, she is already giving
away her power."

BELL HOOKS

"Feminists too often believe that no one has ever experienced
the kind of society that empowered women and made that
empowerment the basis of its rules of civilization. The price
the feminist community must pay because it is not aware of
the recent presence of gynarchical societies on this continent
is unnecessary confusion, division, and much lost time."

PAULA GUNN ALLEN

"In the end, anti-Black, anti-female, and all forms of
discrimination are equivalent to the same thing—
anti-humanism."

SHIRLEY CHISHOLM

"There is one thing you have got to learn about our
movement: Three people are better than no people."

FANNIE LOU HAMER

"Your silence will not protect you."

AUDRE LORDE

"Angry women will change the world."

STREET GRAFFITI IN SOUTH KOREA

"If the struggle of the last decades was against the colonialism that allowed one nation to rule another, the current and future struggle will be about the internal colonialism that allows one race or one sex to dominate another.

"One day our descendants will think it incredible that we paid so much attention to things like the amount of melanin in our skin or the shape of our eyes or our gender instead of the unique identities of each of us as complex human beings."

FRANKLIN THOMAS

If our dreams
weren't already real
within us, we couldn't
even dream them.

NOTES OF GRATITUDE

To say thank you for the presence and pleasure of quotes in my life, I have to start at the beginning.

I thank my mother, Ruth Nuneviller Steinem, for knowing by heart and quoting the words of Edna St. Vincent Millay and Dorothy Parker throughout my childhood. She also woke me up many mornings with these lines from Omar Khayyam:

Awake! for Morning in the Bowl of Night
Has flung the Stone that puts the Stars to Flight.

Later, I understood she had been a writer, too, but had given up her own career years before I was born. How many women are living out the unlived lives of our mothers? And how many sons are living the hopes of their fathers? I look forward to the day when everyone can follow her or his own dreams.

It was also from quotes that I learned there is a special magic to rhyming. Like music, rhyming is a pleasure in itself, even when we don't understand. It made me realize why poets are listened to, even in a different language, and why our own street and song rappers are magic even when we have to listen more than once to understand the words.

This is the first book I've shared with a visual artist, and I'm grateful to Samantha Baker for evoking people and worlds with a few strokes of pen or brush. It's been fun to watch her go beyond language. I also thank Paolo Pepe, the art director of Random House, and designer Simon Sullivan for combining the visual and the verbal.

I thank all the friends and co-conspirators whose words I've also quoted in these pages, and I hope their quotes tantalize readers into finding more of their words. I especially wish Florynce Kennedy, my longtime friend and speaking partner, were here to create quotes for this political era that so needs her. I urge you to read any of the books that are by and about her—she will add to your verbal karate. She also reminds us that the most radical thing any activist can be is understandable.

And I thank the great women in the office that Amy Richards and I share, who checked the accuracy and source of quotes: Amanda McCall, Hannah Cullen, and Blaine Edens. Also my literary agent, Kim Schefler, whose advice was important from the beginning.

Most of all, I want to thank my editor at Random House, Kate Medina, for her patience, generosity, and encouragement. She guides writers not with degrees of criticism, but with ascending degrees of praise. Editors working with her are inspired to do the same, and so this book was shepherded with special care by Erica Gonzalez. This is the kind of support that writers need when putting our words out there for all the world to see.

At the end of this book, there are blank pages for quotes from or found by readers. Wherever we start, on paper or screen or street corner, we are all part of a talking circle.

Gloria Steinem

My Quotes

QUOTES I LOVE

About the Author

GLORIA STEINEM is a writer, political activist, and feminist organizer. She was a founder of *New York* and *Ms.* magazines, and is the author of *My Life on the Road, Moving Beyond Words, Revolution from Within,* and *Outrageous Acts and Everyday Rebellions,* all published in the United States, and *As If Women Matter,* in India. She co-founded the National Women's Political Caucus, the Ms. Foundation for Women, the Free to Be Foundation, and the Women's Media Center in the United States. She also helped found Equality Now, Donor Direct Action, and Direct Impact Africa. For her writing, Steinem has received the Penney-Missouri Journalism Award, the Front Page and Clarion awards, the National Magazine Award, the Lifetime Achievement in Journalism Award from the Society of Professional Journalists, the Society of Writers Award from the United Nations, and the University of Missouri School of Journalism Award for Distinguished Service in Journalism. In 1993, her concern with child abuse led her to co-produce an Emmy Award–winning TV documentary for HBO, *Multiple Personalities: The Search for Deadly Memories.* In 2013, she was awarded the Presidential Medal of Freedom by President Barack Obama. In 2016, she and Amy Richards co-produced a series of eight documentaries on violence against women around the world for VICELAND.

gloriasteinem.com
Facebook.com/GloriaSteinem
Twitter: @GloriaSteinem

About the Illustrator

SAMANTHA DION BAKER is originally from Philadelphia, where she grew up in a family of artists. She graduated from The Cooper Union in New York City and spent over twenty years working as a graphic designer. Now a full-time illustrator and artist, her favorite thing to do is wander the city streets and travel with her family, drawing all of the things she does, eats, and sees, in the pages of her sketch journal. She is the author of *Draw Your Day* and *Draw Your Day Sketchbook*. Samantha lives and works in Brooklyn with her husband and two sons.

sdionbaker.com
Instagram: @sdionbakerdesign